WHERE THE SEA KUNIKS THE LAND

A collection of poetry by Ashley Qilavaq-Savard

Published by Inhabit Media Inc.
www.inhabitmedia.com

Inhabit Media Inc. (Iqaluit) P.O. Box 11125, Iqaluit, Nunavut, X0A 1H0

Editors: Neil Christopher and Anne Fullerton
Art Director: Danny Christopher
Designer: Sam Tse

This project was made possible in part by the Government of Canada.

We acknowledge the support of the Canada Council of Arts for our publishing program.

ISBN: 978-1-77227-444-8

Library and Archives Canada Cataloguing in Publication

Title: Where the sea kuniks the land / a collection of poetry by Ashley Qilavaq-Savard.
Names: Qilavaq-Savard, Ashley, author.
Identifiers: Canadiana 2022042814X | ISBN 9781772274448 (softcover)
Subjects: LCGFT: Poetry.
Classification: LCC PS8633.I53 W44 2022 | DDC C811/.6—dc23

Printed in Canada

WHERE THE SEA KUNIKS THE LAND

A collection of poetry by Ashley Qilavaq-Savard

INHABIT
MEDIA

Contents

I Am an Inuk Woman

I am an Inuk woman
my markings say it so
don't look at me and ask
"taa Inuuviit?"
because I too come from the land of snow and ice
my heart belongs to the place where the sea *kuniks* the land
an Arctic islander on ancient tundra
these histories etched into my roots
these lines filled with familiarity
this identity traced along skin
fighting flames
and
shining stars
from heart to hand
ink to being
chapters readily unfold
these lines are my markings
the story of my journey meant to be told
I walked these lands and know my way home
I washed my sorrows in the river and dried my body in the breeze
I wished for the bitterness of assimilation to stop being so damn easy
I am an Inuk woman
working hard to practise, protect, and preserve the raw beauty of us
as my histories must pass through me in seeds
these lines will welcome the next generation of Inuit
my markings are meant to help me grow
skin and soul

taa Inuuviit? | oh, are you Inuk?
kuniks | kisses given by placing the nose on a person's skin and breathing
in (properly spelled *kuniksaq*)

Arctic Adoration

can you imagine just barely escaping a snowstorm
enough to witness it in all its glory at your tail's end
swallowing whole your home like a
sneaky fox and clueless lemming
swiftly, naturally, unapologetically
suffocating and cleansing all in the same
to feel that fierce wind forcing you into the self-realization of resilience
eyes squinting as a million tiny snowflakes dance so elegantly before you
lungs erupting with crisp clean air, heart outpouring the essence of the
    land
from the most quenching breath, you feel our ancestors flowing through
    your veins
leaving only clarity and vitality as they journey through you

Intergenerational Trauma

it will take me many years to deconstruct
the heavy weight that is buried deep within my roots, before seeds
sprout, this heavy hurt scares growth with intense pains
I never personally experienced
this ever-stunting sorrow is beyond me and my roots
it is so much deeper and so much more horrific than my narrowing
    resentment will allow me to see
comprehending the deep-seeded trauma that is uniquely my own is like
watching the *aqsarniit* dance around the full moon on a cold crisp night
    outside of town
where light pollution does not belong
and to feel for a split second anything but lonely in the dark

aqsarniit | northern lights

Qijuktaaqpait

surrounding myself with white Labrador tea flowers on a dreamlike day
while the breeze hugs my being and the air smells like ocean
is pure joy
I soak up this moment
every song-like sound
every sweet smell swirling about
even the feeling of my hair tickling my face in a gentle loverlike caress
will forever bring me back to this moment when I felt like
Inuuvunga
when my soul was soothed and my skin was smothered in sunkisses

my relationship with the land began before I was born
it is so deeply rooted into who I am
impenetrable, that love,
standing strong in all seasons
you cannot begin to understand who I am if you have never sat silently in
    a field of white Labrador tea flowers and felt wholehearted at home

qijuktaaqpait | Labrador tea
Inuuvunga | I am Inuk / I am alive

My Love and I

my love smells like a forest
and explores my body
gently trekking untouched trails
of the heart
we come together like
still stable stars
and
the awe-inspiring *aqsarniit*
an extraordinary aurora
of body
and
being
my love flows like fresh river water
pure
natural
never ending
admiring the sweetness of my love
is like adoring the sunlight
a feeling so closely linked to happiness
knowing the power of love
brings the body to balance
appreciating the strength of my love
is like building a sturdy home
giving a sense of peace and safety
respecting the intellect of love
opens locked doors with ease
working hard to enrich my love
carries me to unexpected growth
leading me to a meadow of bliss
my eyes observe new ways

of thinking
the ontology
of loving
this human
who has my whole
uummati
hold it gently
with pride
with adoration
with peace
my love feels like the sun on your skin
warm
comforting
bright

aqsarniit | northern lights
uummati | heart

Becoming Whole

I want to feel whole on heavy-hearted broken land
to know my way home during a brazen blizzard
that blinds and pushes and pulls
I want to know in the core that my Inuk identity is untouchable
to feel secure in my roots and build a sanctuary
that shifts and grows and heals
I want to believe in our brightest futures that could last as long as a
    midsummer night's dream
to witness rebirth in multitudes
that protects and centres and reclaims

Gradual Healing

healing does not happen overnight
it can take weeks, years, even decades
it is healing all the same
it cannot quickly cover your soul like frost decorates the world with its
  beautiful delicacy as you sleep
it's a slow accumulation of acceptance of self and situation, adjusting
  perceptions of ambiance and self that must be protected with self-
  compassion and love
recognize the power you carry to heal and all of its forgiving magic
remember there is a difference between thinking that the world is against
  you and when you are against the world
reclaim parts of you that grief had buried in your sorrows
seasons change day by day
slow down love, I say to myself, you are making your way up an enormous
  mountain
a hero's journey happens step by step
you will get there eventually, walk with kindness in your heart while
  comprehending your circumstances, and never losing sight of where
  you are going
a hero's journey is happening

Ever Addicted

Ever addicted.
Ways of bringing peace to never-ending chaos are learned
a withheld secret is how to unlearn assimilation from the mind and body
colonizers don't want you to heal from their continual control
I'll share a secret
the land pulls the heart together long enough that sprouting leaves will
    begin to grow
the ocean air cleanses new growth and gives depth for ideas to move with
    the Arctic wind
to pour down your mountainous mind like fresh rainwater
to sit without the weight of the world
letting go of bad habits to bring your head above water and in the clouds
    feels impossible when you are held down by oppressive systems that
    make it difficult to move let alone think about a future

Mountainous Love

when our lips meet it's like the sun kissing the mountains goodnight
we create the most stunning sunsets
painting the skies with our breathtaking colours
our bodies moving together like the dancing *aqsarniit*
the most extraordinary display of northern lights
as the moon becomes my core, I gravitate towards your salty waters
what a sensation to swim skin to skin in the moonlit ocean with you

aqsarniit | northern lights

Seasonal Depression

it's five a.m. and the snow is softly falling
a thick fleck of intricacy that disappears in the slightest touch of warmth
I happily extend my hand into the dark to catch the tiny pieces of art
and marvel at the peculiar design for what seems like hours, days, and
    weeks
my heart is at ease, rebuilding this moment in my cold body
I am cold, I think, *why isn't it melting*
I wonder at the thought until spring arrives and the thaw begins
the returning sun sheds light into me and warms my core
allowing the snow to melt into my body
absorbing the beautiful art that becomes a part of me

Cycles

I continuously climb out of this hole of survival
I breathe deeply after a hero's journey and relief washes over me
I make my way to thriving, feeling the push from resilience to be more
    than my surroundings and circumstances
I am dragged back in this hole in a horrific fashion, full of fear as my feet
    are pulled out from under me
I reach out to grasp stability, knowing it's a privilege and not a given
I want to be above ground and have my roots search deeply and safely
    down into the histories that have made me who I am
instead I am fully immersed in it all
underground in this hole of survival that has become my second home, if
    not my first
it can feel bleak, empty of joy and full of resentment
decorated with endless worry, senseless anger, and so much pain
I remember the times I made it out with sheer strength and felt the sun
    caressing my face
and the breeze hugging my body
and the world opening up, limitless possibilities for those who are able to
    thrive
and what a privilege it is to do so
this hole of survival splits your spirit into tiny bite-sized pieces because who
    knows how long you'll be stuck here, the troubled rationality that is
    reality
it steals your sense for something better than simply surviving day by day
week by week
year by year goes by as I continuously climb out of this hole again and
    again only to be dragged back

with lost time and lost opportunities, I learn that there is a reason for
everything, even my never-ending hero's journey
growth begins below the surface, even in that place of survival if carefully
treaded
roots are to start and become secure in the deepest of insecurities and
uncertainties
this hole of survival is where the strongest maturation happens
where the stories of my ancestors end and my story begins
if I allow it to flower and listen lightly to the heavy hurt that came before
me
there is power in empathetic insight

Blue

colours are just colours until you find one that speaks to your soul
blue used to be just plain old blue, until I saw a blue so pure and captivating
the seven seas could not compare
to such an alluring siren call that dares me to jump into the icy deep waters
in hope of finding the tiniest glimpse of this all too delicious blue
that has become my compass, in which this blue guides me home
this blue I delightfully drown in fills my very heart to the top
replenishing my soul effortlessly

Holding Grief

if I give my heart to the land, will it hold grief like I do? too tightly and too
    long
it rolls in like thick ice fog in the dead middle of winter
drowning in debilitating delicacy
frost full of fragility
reassure that resilience is resting nearby
waiting for this all too familiar
Nothing feeling to disappear
Nothing feels empty, quiet, seemingly safe
Nothing likes to take time and lose it
more than grief
I don't notice this feeling seeping into my roots
like lifeless dry leaves slowly spreading
decay to Indigenous lineage
I'd never imagined a drought could happen in the Arctic tundra that is my
    home
until I felt it reach my veins, right to my core
I stand staying still as seasons change around me
letting this Nothing become me as I wait for vitality
I learned with wasted time that one does not wait for resilience to be
    awoken
revival of resilience begins with a cry
a release
of sadness
regret
grief
feelings flooding in, not to be drowned in but to replenish and cleanse the
    inner self
I gave my *uummati* to the *nuna*
not to let this all too familiar Nothing consume me

uummati | heart
nuna | land

Lateral Violence

I fade into the background by choice
as my body remembers the pains and repercussions of shining brightly
    during the twenty-four-hour darkness
a light so strong had to be diminished for fear of being taken, or lost
    innocence, they go hand in hand, I think
I am learning that my light should not threaten your being
you become a threat to yourself when you lose your light among my
    aqsarniit soul
I will no longer hold space for those who cannot dance with me under the
    northern lights
I am caught in a crossfire created to keep us quiet, in line, "humble"
and yet our beautiful beings still become stolen sisters, fearful fathers,
    mouthless mothers, and beaten brothers
we lose ourselves in this continual cycle of abuse in the form of
    unaccountability, puffed up pride, and too much hurt unfairly passed
    down
my hurt should not become your hurt, it is solely mine and mine alone, as
    I am responsible for healing the hole in my heart
and to do it with anything less than accountability, a deep understanding
    of why, and complete compassion is letting colonialism win
this hurt did not begin with me, but it will end with me, I am breaking the
    cycle

aqsarniit | northern lights

Burrowed

I want to wash away this worry with the most soothing salt water
drown my cold sorrows while floating above it all
to become a part of the Arctic Ocean and be moved by the current
allowing it to direct my being to tranquility and equanimity
but even in the icy waters, I must remain vigilant of my surroundings, as
    one can never predict a predator or the form in which they follow
one must always expect this natural defense and nature defending itself
for nature is all in all its naturalness
days like these create a rooted yearning to burrow underneath tundra, to
    encompass the soil, rock, and permafrost
and await maturation and deepen my roots across this land, this *nuna* that
    is my home and my being
I crave so deeply the traditional knowledge that colonialism has stolen, my
    rightful heritage borrowed by time
the clock is ticking I worry, too much time has passed as our fervid
    knowledge-holding Elders linger longingly for knowledge-hungry youth
our Elders, the gatekeepers that hold so tenderly our ancestral world, keep
    them safe as we need them more than the land itself

nuna | land

Skins

what a glory feeling it is to sit in the sun by the oceanside
as *tulugait* and *naujait* sing circling above
and scrape skins with centuries of *arnait* guiding my *ulu*
an intimate relationship develops from skin to skin
an intergenerational transmission of traditional knowledge
an ideological shift in relations with the *sila*
the processes of pure ingenuity and the utmost respect for all
from birth to babe to the ultimate end

I imagine the journey of this particular seal
reaching for the last breath
and all the journeys before that
creation's circle,
a life lived
an ending of sorts
a beginning of traditions
an innermost relationship blossoms
a deep appreciation of those before

I can feel the elation and gratitude from the young hunter
as the act of melting snow in one's mouth
the first of many to come
from fresh *imiq* transferred mouth to mouth
a long-established tradition of giving the seal a last drink begins
keeping the survival of livelihood breathing crisp Arctic air

tulugait | ravens
naujait | seagulls
arnait | women
ulu | crescent knife traditionally used by women
sila | weather
imiq | water

as I tend to my *qisik*
I pull my skin over the *avvik*
scraping off the future oil for my *qulliq*
I marvel at our ingenuity as Inuit
our ability to make use of anything and everything around us
my ulu guides a shedding of grief
a loss of language and relation to land in the midst of being discovered
a removal of sorrow
a rendering of warmth in the purest form
to saturate summer's harvest of *maniq* and *suputiit*
fusing together a bright future

I am guided by centuries of *arnait*
my mother, my grandmother, my great-grandmother
generations of strong and capable Inuit women who came before me
my body is remembering the strength within and the peace to know
    oneself
a connection nurtured by empathic insight

qisik | sealskin pelt
avvik | the board used to scrape fat and membrane off animal skins
qulliq | seal oil lamp
maniq | lamp moss—mixed with suputiit to use as wick for qulliq
suputiit | Arctic willow—mixed with maniq to use as wick for qulliq

Crushing

it is easier to detach from self than to feel the world collapse around you,
    it's a catch-22
why do I only matter once I overcome adversity?

every soul-shattering event cannot sneak up on you if you run fast enough,
    my spirit tired of feeling broken
why am I only wanted when I'm whole and turned away when I'm not?

if I struggle, I become inconvenient, easily forgotten, as do all of our
    struggling Indigenous youth
why do we turn a blind eye to those who need it most?

life seems manageable when you cannot feel the grief of losing our stolen
    sisters, fearing erasure of identity and culture, all on top of deep-seeded
    colonial trauma
we are stuck in a system not built for us, it is no wonder we walk around
    snow-blinded into our ever-changing world that we have little say in
yet we are expected to navigate with grace, civility, and a stiff upper lip
    against violated treaties and continual colonial control

as a young Indigenous woman, I carry two worlds on my shoulders
without support systems in place to help carry the immense weight and
    heavy hurt
it is no wonder I turned to debilitating habits
I am pulling myself out of grief
out of pain
out of hopelessness
that takes bravery and courage I never knew I held
because it's bravery and courage that do not belong to me originally
but what is gifted to all of us through our ancestors' histories and lineage

Tuktu

I like the way windy snow dances like a thousand caribou running freely on
    the man-made paved road
such a strange sight
nature so fierce and delicate
natural on top of unnatural
light matter on heavy-hearted broken land
maybe it's a beacon of hope, for the undeniable force of nature that
    surrounds us
or maybe it's a token of the past, showing our generation what great herds of
    tuktu once looked like
I saw a herd once
large, strong, and healthy
caribou peacefully eating lichen and resting on the other side of the Sylvia
    Grinnell River
the roaring river was no match for my hungry stomach
growling with greed
crying for caribou
I turned to my mother and said, "Tell Pauloosie to get his gun." There was
    no asking, only telling
she just laughed, because my bossy six-year-old behaviour was less common
    and more comedic than the moment before us
I could not fathom such mundane mentality towards such succulent
    creatures
in time I learned that it was not for the lack of love of *tuktuminiq*, but the
    respect and love of tuktu
it took me many years to comprehend the connection that comes from
    respecting all forms of life
and their contributions to your life
the *nuna* and all of its seemingly bounty-less bounty
lessons are to be learned on the land and from the land

tuktu | caribou
tuktuminiq | caribou meat
nuna | land

Dance with Me

will you dance with me like the wind and snow do during a brazen
    blizzard?
mending together body and soul in a whimsical whirl
I am drawn to you like a *malikkaat* flower follows the warm sun
you are the warm sun and cool breeze on the most dreamlike of
    Greenlandic sunny summer days
the wonderland where I found you in all its radiance
you are nature at its finest, embracing changing seasons and breathing
    colour to life like the Torngat Mountains' heartfelt tundra during
    Labrador's most lively fall
you are the strongest river *siku* with the purest essence flowing underneath
    those icy blue eyes
I could happily drink you up for years to come as long as you'll share your
    ambrosian love with me

malikkaat | mountain aven flower
siku | ice

My Second Mother

my sister is like a second mother to me

as our mother fought battles we could not comprehend, my sister was instinctively tending to our war wounds with such attentiveness

she prepared bottles of powdered milk and changed diapers in her half-asleep daze, she was eight years old when her body learned to do these things for our baby brother

eldest children often take on such responsibilities without ever having been asked, they just do

my brave sister takes on the world with such strength and resilience, even from the day she was prematurely born, forcing her way into this life on no one else's agenda but her own

a true fighter that one

she holds a fire so intense, it often attracts cold characters looking for warmth

she shares her fierce flame in a campfire kind of way, bringing community together and making everyone feel seen and heard

eldest daughters often are like second mothers

my second mother held me in her arms and protected me as if I was her own flesh and blood, I guess you can say I am as we are the same flesh and blood through and through

she taught me the true value of hard work, perseverance, and resilience

I would not be who I am and all that I love about myself without her

I am strong because of her

my caring soul was bottle-fed by her loving heart

My Mother Fought Colonial Oppression

my mother taught me that strength does not only look like confidence in
    spades
her strength came from fighting an oppressive system blinded by capitalism
a system not made by Inuit or for Inuit
she fought tirelessly day in and day out to ensure her growing children did
    not starve
she gave us the food meant for her mouth to make sure our bellies were
    satisfied
although it left her without
witnessing this was a gift and a given
we did not have the world handed to us
if anything the threat of everything collapsing around us was our world
    growing up
that is how oppression works
it keeps you busy climbing out of poverty,
dangerous and scary situations
along with essential resources withheld time and time again
it is simply surviving day by day when society only rewards those who thrive
oppressed people struggle to survive, they are often misunderstood and
    mistreated
it is easier to put on the blindfold that is privilege
than to witness injustice and dismantle oppressive systems
my mother showed us the world for what it really is
and taught me that true strength, the kind that goes unnoticed and
    unappreciated, is strengthening others, even in moments of immense
    weakness
she taught me to appreciate all that I have and to give when I can
I am strong because of her
my resilience stems from her core

Help

I do not need your help
my people are suffering
because we are ignored
I do not need your help
my people are starving
because we are forgotten
I do not need your help
my people are dying
because you can't admit
that you poisoned us
I do not need your help
my people are losing
their culture, themselves
because you couldn't
embrace our way of life
a life is a life
precious as is
let it live
I do not need your help
I do not want your help

I do not want your help
my people are strong
it's in our blood
I do not want your help
my people are caring
it's in our values
I do not want your help
my people are resilient
it's in every bit of our being

we are without question
I do not want your help
my people are taking back
what was once forbidden
it's our identity
our history
our heritage
we will take it back
pass it down
let it live
I do not need your help
I do not want your help
I need your support

I need your support
to accept our differences
you expect us to accept yours
I need your support
to appreciate our people
we belong just as much
I need your support
to admit your mistakes
identity cannot be banned
I need your support
to see that we are suffering
because we are ignored
forgotten
poisoned
lost
strong

caring
resilient
because we are Indigenous
see that we are also human beings
I need your support
to help regain our identity
invest, protect, accept
I need your support
to help our people
killing a culture
can kill a person
I need your support
to help our youth feel complete
do not steal their sense of self
I need your support
to help our land and sea
our home is sacred
it is our reason for being
we will rise
we will prevail
we will live

About the Author

Ashley Qilavaq-Savard is an Inuk artist, writer, and emerging filmmaker born and raised in Iqaluit, Nunavut.

Since attending the Vancouver Film School, Ashley has led acting and storytelling workshops for children and youth with the Qaggiavuut Performing Arts Society and the Labrador Creative Arts Festival. As a storyteller and spoken word performer, she has performed at the St. John's Storytelling Festival 2018, and across Inuit Nunangat and Greenland with Adventure Canada.

Ashley has published two short stories relating to her Inuit culture, "My Very First Ulu" with *Nipiit* magazine and "Miki and the Aqsarniit" with *Chirp* magazine. Ashley also writes poetry about decolonizing narratives, healing from intergenerational trauma, and love of the land and culture.

Ashley creates sealskin and beaded jewellery and accessories for women and men, celebrating and educating on the importance of sealskin and Inuit sustainable seal hunting. She is also a dedicated student of Inuktitut, and is a full-time student in the Aurniarvik program at the Pirurvik Centre, working towards her certificate in Indigenous Language Proficiency from the University of Victoria.

Glossary of Inuktut Words

Inuktut is the word for Inuit languages spoken in Canada, including Inuktitut and Inuinnaqtun. The pronunciation guides in this book are intended to support non-Inuktut speakers in their reading of Inuktut words. These pronunciations are not exact representations of how the words are pronounced by Inuktut speakers.

For more resources on how to pronounce Inuktut words, visit inhabitmedia.com/inuitnipingit.

WORD	PRONUNCIATION	DEFINITION
aqsarniit	ahq–sahr–NEET	northern lights
arnait	ahr–NAH–EET	women
avvik	AH–veek	the board used to scrape fat and membrane off animal skins
imiq	EE–meek	water
Inuuvunga	EE–NOO–voo–ngah	I am Inuk / I am alive
kuniks	KOO–neeks	kisses given by placing the nose on a person's skin and breathing in (properly spelled *kuniksaq*)
malikkaat	MAH–lee–KAAT	mountain aven flower
maniq	MAH–neek	lamp moss—mixed with suputiit to use as wick for qulliq
naujait	nah–ooh–YAHT	seagulls
nuna	NOO–nah	land
qijuktaaqpait	kee–yook–TAHK–pah–eet	Labrador tea
qisik	KEE–seek	sealskin pelt
qulliq	KOO–leek	seal oil lamp
siku	SEE–koo	ice
sila	SEE–lah	weather
suputiit	soo–POO–teet	Arctic willow—mixed with maniq to use as wick for qulliq
taa Inuuvit?	tah I–NOO–veet?	oh, are you Inuk?
tuktu	TOOK–tu	caribou
tuktuminiq	TOOK–too–mee–neek	caribou meat
tulugait	too–loo–GAH–eet	ravens
ulu	OO–loo	crescent knife traditionally used by women
uummati	OOM–mah–tee	heart

INHABIT
MEDIA